POP ME A POEM

Dominic R. Daniels

Dedicated to
All Young Souls Who Dream of Wonders and to the Young at Heart

This little collection of children's poems was written long ago when I was but a child myself in the very early years of my youth. I was 12 years old.

Personal
Dedication to:
Phil and Mary Daniels
Minoy Lee
Al Little
Theresa Lucy Macedonia
Marina Hanson
Dr. James Golden
Betty June Nelson

CHRISTMAS

There was smell of Christmas in the air tonight.
There was a thought
What did Christmas smell like?
Like ham and turkey and honey.

And if you wondered what Christmas sounded like.
It sounded like bells ringing and people singing
And the snow falling from the sky and Santa.

And going further, what did Christmas look like?
Like sleigh's riding on the snow or it looked like a toy store, bundling gifts,
trains, porcelain china dolls, hot rod cars, and video games for good little
boys and girls. Or a bakery with piping hot tasty treats all crispy and good
to eat. Or a classic Christmas movie or cartoon, the kind that would make
you snuggle next to a cozy fire and snooze into dreams.

That was how Christmas smelled and looked and sounded. And tonight you could almost touch and feel Christmas.

CUPCAKES

Cupcakes are cool and cupcakes are neat, they make you jump, and they are good for a holiday treat.

Cupcakes are chocolaty and so sweet; they are the best of all junk food sweets.

Cupcakes are good at parties because it's even tastier with candy sweet tarts.

But most of all I think that if you're going to eat cupcakes, eat also some healthy treats.

COMETS

Comets are big and comets are small. They sound like thunder when they fall and blunder. Comets are great to see in books just like how the scientists go and look.

Astronomers see many stars, but not comets because they're really far out in outer space. Like the moons of Jupiter and the red spot on its face.

Comets make crashes loud as the bombs blast and make you shudder. They make you jump and run and scream.

Comets are fun when they shoot through the sky, just make a wish and your dreams will come true just like mine.

CATS

Cats are playful and very fun. Cats are soft and cute to pet and they barely have to go see the vet. Cats are cuddly and cats are gentle they are harmless like bunny rabbits.

Cats make excellent pets to have because they don't make big, big, big messes. They are clean to kiss and fluffy to pet.

Cats like milk and cream because of the rich flavor that makes it go easy down their little tummies. Cats like fish and a little bit of meat so watch out you rascal mice, you are next up to eat.

I think cats are very good pets because most of all cats like people who love cats for pets.

CEREAL

Cereals are cold and cereals are hot. It tastes so you good that you go hyper. Sugar sweet puffs make you jump and freak. Healthy cereal has no game, yet it wakes up the brain to help you think clearly to start your day.

It is good to eat a balanced meal so that you will stay strong as metal, steel and be tough in school to fight all your worries just like beating up those baddie bullies.

Eat your cereal everyday and you'll go big and strong like a fighting machine.

FRUIT

Fruit is healthy and the fruit is sweet. It makes such a delicious treat.

Fruit is always such a beautiful thing because fruit like the apple, is a teacher's precious jewel.

The fruit gives you vitamin C and minerals that you may need.

Best of all is it gives your body lots of speedy fast energy.

I AM ANNE FRANK

I am Anne Frank.
I wonder about if I will live through the war.
I hope the war ends soon.
I dream of candy and ice cream.
I remember riding my bike.
I believe I will survive.
I am Anne Frank.

I fear for my family's lives.
I hate eating beans.
I worry about the Jews that are hurt.
I cry when I'm sad.
I am Anne Frank.

I think about before the war started.
I feel very lonely.
I see in my mind my future.
I hear about the complaints of Mrs. Van Daan.
I understand how my life is now.
I am Anne Frank.

JUST BECAUSE I AM NOT POPULAR

Just because I'm not popular,
I'm not a nerd or some genius,
Just because I'm not popular,
Doesn't mean that I'm a loner
Or that I don't have any friends.
Just because you like sports doesn't mean that I don't.

Just because my parents drive nice cars, doesn't mean that I'm rich or a
snob.
Just because I joke around at times doesn't make me a jerk or unkind.

I am not trendy or ignorant,
I am not a loser,
I am myself and like no one else.
I am an artist and a free thinker.
I really try to be kind to others.
Give me a chance toward being a friend and you'll find someone different
that what you saw on the outside.

MOTHERS DAY

Mother's Day is a special time of the year when children come to thank and honor their mother's by helping them out more in their chores.

Writing a Mother's Day card, giving their mother's a gift of thanks, showing respect and obedience.

Mother's Day is when you thank your mother for every kind and good teaching they taught you: good morals, good behavior and other things.

Mother's Day is when you especially thank your mother for taking care of you when you're sick and lonely. But most of all that I would like to say is that our mothers are in our lives every day.

ROSES

Roses are red. Violets are blue. The same to me, I'll write to you.
Roses are fun to plant and smell because they remind me of the cardinals
in the garden.
Roses are pretty and lovely to sell, but some of them I couldn't tell.

Roses are great for springtime fun, because they make you dance, laugh,
and sing in the springtime sun.

But best of all roses I think are beautiful, lovely, gentle, and neat. Reddish
as scarlet hearts that burn with passion and jump with beats. They make
you happy to give to your mom or a girlfriend. For love and for cheer, to
give kindness to a sick friend or someone dear.

MY DAD

My Dad is a special dad because he takes me on vacation to distant lands.
Helps me wash the dishes.
Helps me solve my problems with the school bullies.

I give him hugs and kisses for who he is.
He puts food on the table.
He shelters us with a loving home.
He takes us to restaurants, sometimes when my mom is too busy to cook.
He cheers me up when I am lonely and tells me funny jokes.
He tucks me in bed, so I will be warm, and I won't be afraid.
He tells me of his old childhood memories when he played baseball and how well he did in school.
Every Day, all the time, every year to the end of time my Dad will be near.

THANKSGIVING

Thanksgiving is the time of the year when people are thankful for God's blessings given to them throughout the year.

Thanksgiving is the time of year when turkeys are cooked and harvesting time is near for making the trimmings like sweet yummy pumpkin pie and candied yams eat and to prepare.

Thanksgiving is the time of year when families come together and share the memories and activities and their relative's care.

Thanksgiving is the time of the year when pilgrims came to the New World and make friends with the Indians to have peace and land to share.

But most of all Thanksgiving is the time of year when everyone is celebrating the Thanksgiving holiday everywhere.

TREASURE

Treasures are hidden everywhere and they shine with bright glare, that you will find in the sea, trees and riches of golden glee.

Treasures are many things that you can see, like the books you read and stories you can write about.

Treasures could be your family's love for you and me.

Treasures could be the fish in the sea, family pets, or planting trees.

Treasures could be your favorite subject because you like to learn as much knowledge as you need.

Treasures could be having fun memories, going to the games, your first kiss, or the movies you've seen.

But finally treasures could be anything you want and think of in your dreams.

WARRIOR

I am a warrior riding through the wind and trees, shooting arrows at the enemy ghouls with shadowy wings.
Fighting hundreds of warlords with clanking swords, sharp as steel.
Pounding them down with sludge hammers on their knees.
Crushing their bones to dust with a great victory.
I am a warrior of the spirit and soul, of the night, water, air, fire, earth and the universe in hand to hold.
Storm and flames in the human soul, burn bright, burn true, burn great, burn with delight, burn with the power that Heaven has placed in you, that you may gain wisdom and deep spiritual insight.

WINTER

Winter is the coldest of days
Then it snows when you're about to play.
You can make a snowman and have snowball fights during all the day.

Winter is the coldest of days.
It is the time when you cuddle in the freezing cold, and you have to huddle.
You drink hot coco because it keeps you warm and from going loco.

Winter is the coldest of days. You sit in front of a fire and pet your cat,
watch TV and then you retire.

Winter is the coldest of days.
You're snug in bed sleeping with your dog when he should be in the shed.
But most of all, I would like to say that winter is truly the coldest of days.

ANGELS

Angels are good and angels are bad
Angels guide us through the hot winds and the sands of time
Angels are in paintings and pictures of all kinds, showing us their marvel-
ous deeds of miraculous zeal.
Angels bring news of joy and Jesus' birth and His glory that shines.
Angels sing praises of hymns that the newborn Christ's journey begins.
Some of the Angels are Saints and Protectors of the Innocent.
Warriors and slayers of devils and evil beasts.
The Arch Angel Michael, the great general and prince of Heavens' armies.
Angels were there on the first Easter morning, when the Lord of All Host,
Christ Jesus rose from the grave.
The Angels proclaim the power of God for the glory of God.
They guard us and protect us, each night and each day. Rain or shine, they
watch over us, in all ages, in all times.
Servants of God to protect and serve all mankind.

BASEBALL

Baseball is the game of sluggers and champions of the leagues
A manly game where you hit home runs and steal a few bases
While in the crowd you gorge down a chili dog and wipe clean your faces
Shout to the vendor for a bag of salty peanuts while you guzzle down a root
beer and when it's the third inning you go nuts!
Babe Ruth would be proud, nothing like going down the old ball game, such
a grand experience on a fine summer day.
The grandstands are filled with the roaring crowds, of the young and old.
Baseball, an American past time that never will fade away, but will always
shine bright like the dawn of a new day.

DOUGHNUTS

Doughnuts are sugar filled and very sweet.
Such a frosty and tasty treat.
Flavors and cakes of all kinds, deep fried in oil and lovely grease.
Everyone's guilty pleasure, but a little boy's dessert of delight.
Apple Fritters, Long Johns, Twists, Bars, Jelly filled stuffed and don't forget
Glazed.
Doughnuts with nuts and chocolate sprinkles, powdered sugar and pink
sweet cakes.
Good o'le buttermilk and old fashioned is chewy and fluffy but not a mess
to ingest.
Junk food heaven for the body to inhale and intake.

NONA

Nona is the Italian word for Grandmother.
Nona Theresa
My dear grandmother, ever sweet and loving.
Feisty and stubborn, a good cook and wonderful seamstress
Nona, she is a good storyteller as many Italian grannies are.
Old wives tales and superstition is with them, but truth in the old tales can
come about.
Tales of white witches, fairies and forests filled with dangerous monsters
and powerful heroes, ancient nursery rhythms and riddles.
To my Nona, the caretaker of the house, spoiler of grandchildren and a
patient as a little mouse.
Smart and full of wit and plenty of charm. I will always love you my grand-
mother, wherever you are.

POTATOES

Potatoes are starchy vegetables, spuds cooked fine as French Fries, a hedonist and food lover's pleasure.
Tasty for a snack, add some salt and some red pepper.
A spice that is nice
Good with cheeseburgers, fair food that everyone loves to eat.
Slice them and cooked the peels thin in a frying pan with olive oil, serve it with baked or fried cod fish with a little saucer of tartar sauce that will enhance the taste.
A great meal for Good Friday before Easter takes place.

VALENTINES DAY

What is Valentine's Day?
Lots of hugs and chocolate kisses
Young couples dancing and singing
A time for marriage and time of peace
A time for deep passion and sharing kind thoughts and helpful deeds
Love birds chirping gracefully
Roses sold in flower shops with a brown teddy bear newly stuffed
Red ribbons and pink greeting cards to share sentiments with care
An enjoyable night to share a romantic dinner, under the twinkling stars
and by glowing candlelight.
For little children and young people like me, parties and class picnics, a
day off and a day to relax.
A brief moment we live in a special holiday that comes just but once a year,
but a feeling and the lesson that is dear.
Always be kind and loving to others, for in return you will find it rewarding.

THE CIRCUS

The Circus is a wonderful place to be, to escape, to run wild and ever so free. In that dreamy like place, there are so many oddities to see. Rides to ride and games to play.

Take home a prize for your girl and save the day, a kiss for luck and a kiss for the win.

Step right up, test your strength, hit the top of the meter with the wooden mallet and be the worlds' strongest man you can be.

Ride the roller coaster, steal a romantic moment in the tunnel of love, have a thrill on the hammerhead while your stomach churns, play some dart games and pop some balloons.

Enjoy the carnival and the circus of dreams; it is a rare place where childhood lives many great fantasies.

The time of teenage years will soon come, so enjoy these sacred moments of youth whenever the opportunity may arise, life comes and goes fast during our time.

ABOUT THE AUTHOR

About the Author: Born Dominic Rocky Daniels, in the city of Anaheim, California in 1984, he was raised in San Gabriel, CA. At a young age his passion has always been in films, animation, and storytelling. He is best known for his dark fantasy / vampire book series: *The Damascus Chronicles (Book 1)* & *The Damascus Chronicles: Denizens of the Night (Book 2)*, which has won the *Amazon Editors Choice Award: Best Books of 2014*.

Trained in fine art at the age of 10, he decided to go into the entertainment business and become a writer. He is a self-taught author and electronic dance music arranger under his Nega Blast X music production brand. He has a Bachelor Degree of Science in Media Arts and Animation from The Art Institute of California-Los Angeles. In his spare time he reads graphic novels and studies movies, his favorite music is heavy metal.

www.ingramcontent.com/pod-product-compliance
Lightning Source LLC
Chambersburg PA
CBHW060648030426
42337CB00018B/3511